Nelson Is Kidnapped

Story by Beverley Randell
Illustrations by Julian Bruère

When Nelson the baby elephant was six months old, the wet season arrived. Nelson had never seen rain before. Dark gray clouds filled the sky, and rain poured down, day after day.

The dry river beds filled and became swamps. Every time Nelson took a step, the water splashed up. He loved sloshing through this new wet world.

When the rainy season ended, the grass on the flat plain grew tall and strong. All the African animals had plenty to eat. Many elephant families walked a long way to get their share of the new grass.

Wherever Nelson looked, he could see families of elephants.

There were large elephants and small elephants, old elephants and young elephants, cross elephants and kind elephants.

Nelson had the time of his life. He kept running up to strange elephants and smelling them with his little trunk. He wanted to play.

It was fun to find another baby elephant and play pushing games. The other elephant would push back with its head, and soon they would find out who was stronger. Nelson loved these games.

Nelson's big sister Nina had a hard job looking after him. She didn't want her little brother to get lost, or scared, or hurt.

One morning, Nelson ran up to a new family of large elephants. He could not see any young elephants to play with, but the big ones seemed friendly. They dropped their trunks on his back and nudged him beside their legs. They felt him all over. Then the oldest elephant in the family pulled him right underneath her with her strong trunk.

But when Nelson tried to move away, she would not let him go! He pushed and struggled, but he could not escape. The other elephants in the family moved in and blocked his way. He was surrounded.

Nelson was a prisoner behind a solid fence of legs. He had been kidnapped!

Nelson could not understand what was happening, and he was terrified. No matter where he tried to go, legs blocked his way. He began to squeal and tears filled his eyes.

Nina heard his cries of fear, and hurried to help him. When she came close, she saw that the elephants were holding Nelson in a cage of legs. She tried to reach him, but she got a poke in her side from a sharp tusk! It hurt!

It was clear that the other elephants wanted to keep Nelson and make him **their** baby! Nina could not rescue him by herself, so she ran back to her own family for help. She squealed to let them know that something was very wrong.

Then Nelson's mother, and one of his aunts, followed Nina. When they saw Nelson they tried to get him back, but the other elephants turned on them, too. They poked Nelson's mother in the side with their tusks. They would not let her get anywhere near her baby.

The kidnappers were large and strong and there were more of them. Nelson's mother and his aunt and his big sister Nina were very distressed. Nelson was **theirs**! If the strange family took him away, he would die. He needed his mother's milk.

Nelson's wise old grandmother decided what to do. She stepped forward and made a rumbling call. Nelson's mother came and stood beside her, so that their sides touched. Then all the fully grown elephants in Nelson's family hurried to join them. Together they made a broad row that was going to charge to the rescue.

The six elephants, shoulder to shoulder, moved toward the kidnappers. Their great white tusks faced forward. The ground shook under their heavy feet as they advanced.

When the kidnappers saw all of Nelson's family charging toward them, they tried to stand firm. But then they were pushed hard by six determined elephants, all shoving together!

The kidnappers were forced to take a few steps back. As they moved their legs, a gap appeared. Nelson saw the space, squeezed through, and escaped!

Shaking with fright, he ran straight to his mother. Then all his family hurried away with Nelson safely among them. They made happy trumpeting noises as they went, and the kidnappers just stood and watched them go.

Nelson's family had won the battle.

And after that, although he still loved to play pushing games with **small** elephants, Nelson knew that it was wise to keep out of the way of strange **large** elephants.

Nelson had learned a lesson he would never forget.